To

Magnificent
Doctor
Milligan

Your magnificence
has been
recognised e
loved.

Doctrilla
XXX

ME
WITHOUT
YOU...

...IS LIKE
SKY WITHOUT
BLUE

summersdale

ME WITHOUT YOU

Summersdale Publishers Ltd
46 West Street
Chichester
West Sussex
PO19 1RP
UK

www.summersdale.com

Printed and bound in China

ISBN: 978-1-84953-129-0

Substantial discounts on bulk quantities of Summersdale books are available to corporations, professional associations and other organisations. For details contact Summersdale Publishers by telephone: +44 (0) 1243 771107, fax: +44 (0) 1243 786300 or email: nicky@summersdale.com.

TO ....

FROM ....

ME WITHOUT YOU

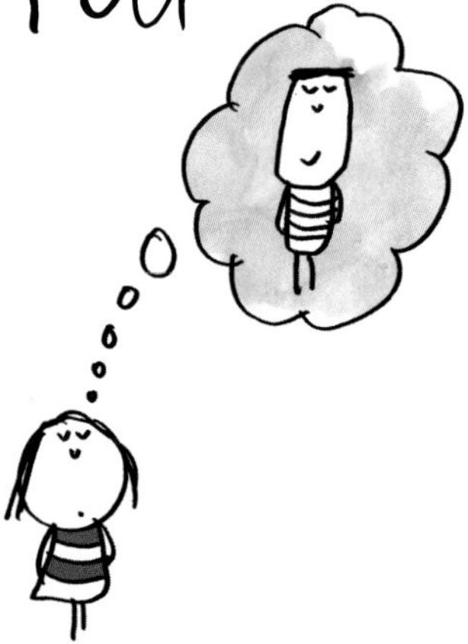

ME
WITHOUT
YOU
IS LIKE...

HAIR
WITHOUT
DO

RESTAURANT
WITHOUT
MENU

ESKIMO
WITHOUT
IGLOO

KUNG
WITHOUT
FU

BIKER
WITHOUT

TATTOO

GHOST
WITHOUT
BOO

MORNING
WITHOUT
DEW

COW
WITHOUT
MOO

DOVE
WITHOUT
COO

TANGO
WITHOUT
TWO

PARTY
WITHOUT
YAHOO!

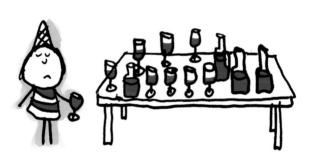

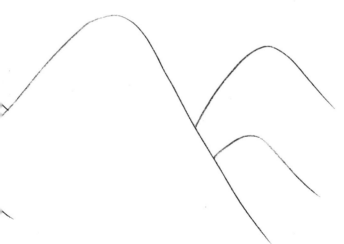

PEAK
WITHOUT
VIEW

MUCH
WITHOUT
ADO

HARRY
WITHOUT
YOU-KNOW-WHO

BORED
BORED
BORED

OAR
WITHOUT
CANOE

KANGA
WITHOUT
ROO

OCH AYE
WITHOUT THE
NOO

OCH,
AYE

CHIMNEY
WITHOUT
FLUE

CLOCK
WITHOUT
CUCKOO

CAT
WITHOUT
MEW

IRISH
WITHOUT
STEW

FOOT
WITHOUT
SHOE

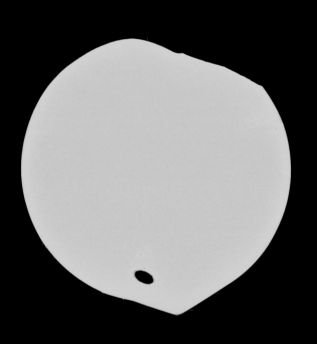

DETECTIVE
WITHOUT A
CLUE

WRECK
WITHOUT
RESCUE

SHOOBEE
WITHOUT
DOO

PENNY WITHOUT A
CHEW

ZOO
WITHOUT
GNU

HOW
WITHOUT
DO-YOU-DO?

ANTIQUE
WITHOUT
VALUE

RAINBOW
WITHOUT
HUE

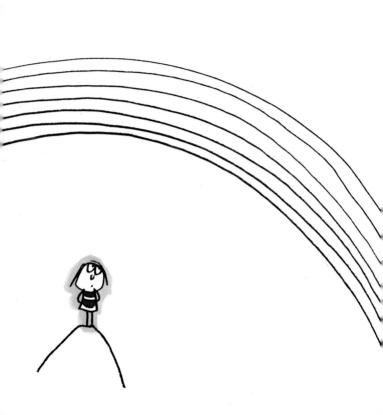

TEA
WITHOUT
BREW

PICNIC
WITHOUT
LOO

BELLS
WITHOUT
BLUE

COCK
WITHOUT A
DOODLE-DO

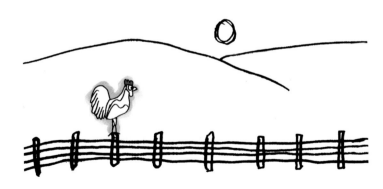

SNOOKER WITHOUT A CUE

SHOW
WITHOUT
QUEUE

MOWGLI
WITHOUT
BALOO

A WITCH WITHOUT HER BREW

A COOK
WITHOUT HIS
SOUS

SNEEZE
WITHOUT A-

A-A-A--

TCHOO.

DISCIPLE
WITHOUT
GURU

POTTY
WITHOUT
POO

COLD
FONDUE

PANDA
WITHOUT
BAMBOO

RUMBLE
RUMBLE

A PICTURE
THAT'S
ASKEW

A FLAT
KAZOO

A NON-SPICY
VINDALOO

A KNOT
I CAN'T
UNDO

BOO

HOO

HOO

HOOOOOOOOOOooo

ME
WITHOUT
YOU!?

WHAT
WOULD I
DO?

BOO!

PHEW!

FOR EMMALINA

Have you enjoyed this book? If so, why not write a
review on your favourite website?

Thanks very much for buying this
Summersdale book.

www.summersdale.com